Get Ready For
Kindergarten

★ NUMBERS, TIME & OPPOSITES ★

Math

Days and Months

Comparing

Numbers 1–20

Telling Time

More than 100 stickers

Heather Stella

BLACK DOG
& LEVENTHAL
PUBLISHERS

ISBN: 978-1-57912- 938-5

Library of Congress Cataloging-in-Publication Data on file
at the offices of Black Dog & Leventhal Publishers, Inc.

Manufactured in the United States

Published by
Black Dog & Leventhal Publishers, Inc.
151 West 19th Street
New York, New York 10011

Distributed by
Workman Publishing Company
225 Varick Street
New York, New York 10014

h g f e d c b

Contents

1, 2, 3, and 4

Practice writing numbers.

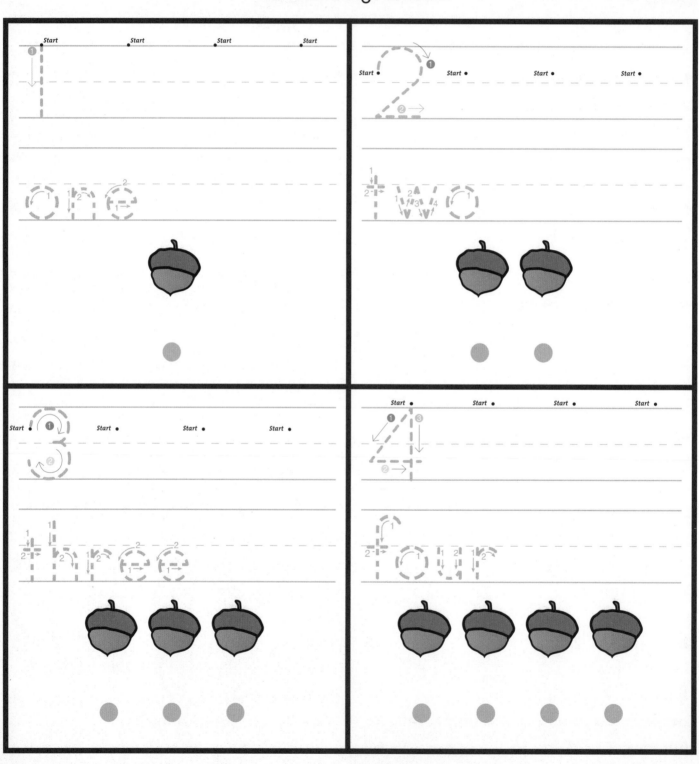

1, 2, 3, and 4

Tally marks are used to count or keep score. They are grouped in sets of five, which makes counting faster. Each **I** mark equals 1. After there are four **I** marks, a **/** mark crosses through them, which equals five.

1		6	⊥⊥⊥⊥ I
2	II	7	⊥⊥⊥⊥ II
3	III	8	⊥⊥⊥⊥ III
4	IIII	9	⊥⊥⊥⊥ IIII
5	⊥⊥⊥⊥	10	⊥⊥⊥⊥ ⊥⊥⊥⊥

Count the tally marks and circle the correct number.

1　2　3　4　　　　　　　1　2　3　4

Ordinal Numbers

Circle the 2ⁿᵈ tree. Draw a line under the 4ᵗʰ tree.

Circle the number of fish in each bowl.

1　2　3　4　　　　　　　1　2　3　4

1　2　3　4　　　　　　　1　2　3　4

SKIP COUNT BY.
2's.
SAY THE NUMBERS OUT LOUD.

2
4

Same Size

Look at the picture of the sports ball in each row. Circle the picture of the ball in each row that is the **same size** as the first picture.

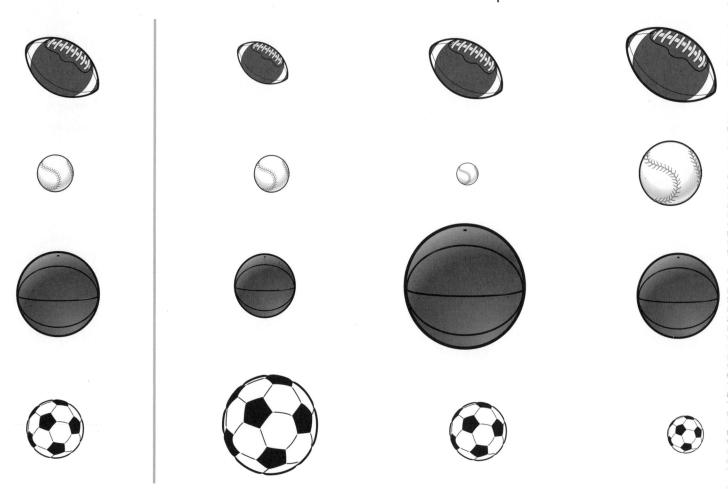

Draw the triangle in the box the exact same size as the orange triangle.

Look at the picture of the birds in each row. Circle the picture of the bird in each row that is a **different size** than the first picture.

Telling Time

A clock shows 12 hours, which is half a day. Fill in the missing hours.

Telling Time

Look at the hands on each clock. Then color in the box with the correct time.

2:00
3:00

5:00
6:00

9:00
11:00

12:00
2:00

1:00
3:00

10:00
9:00

minute hand (long)

hour hand (short)

Done!

5, 6, 7, and 8

Practice writing numbers.

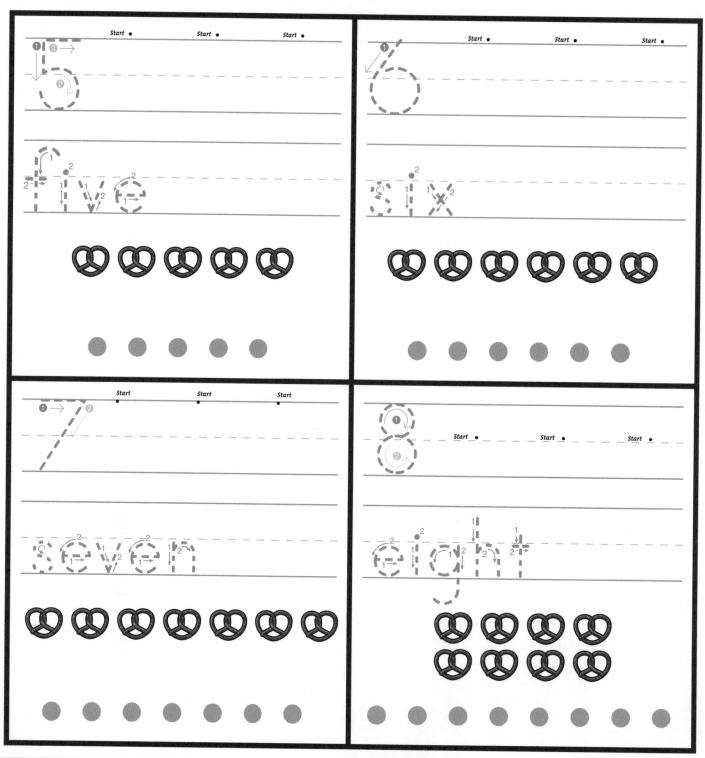

5, 6, 7, and 8

Done!

Tally marks are used to count or keep score. They are grouped in sets of five, which makes counting faster. Each **I** mark equals 1. After there are four **I** marks, a **/** mark crosses through them, which equals five.

1	 I	6	ЖЖ I
2	II	7	ЖЖ II
3	III	8	ЖЖ III
4	IIII	9	ЖЖ IIII
5	ЖЖ	10	ЖЖ ЖЖ

Count the tally marks and circle the correct number.

ЖЖ II   ЖЖ

5 6 7 8   5 6 7 8

Ordinal Numbers

Circle the 5th elephant. Draw a line under the 7th elephant.

Count the balls in each row. Draw a line to the matching number.

          8

         6

    **7**

           5

SKIP COUNT BY.

2's.

SAY THE NUMBERS OUT LOUD.

2

4

6

8

Bigger and Smaller

Look at the animals in each box and color in the one that is **bigger**.

Look at the animals in each box and color in the one that is **smaller**.

 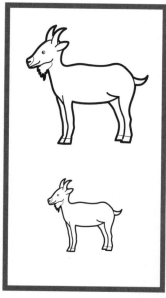  

Bigger and Smaller

Number the items 1, 2, or 3 from smallest to biggest.

Done!

Days of the Week

Each day of the week has its own name. It begins with a capital letter.
There are 7 days in the week in this order:

Sunday	**M**onday	**T**uesday	**W**ednesday	**T**hursday	**F**riday	**S**aturday
1	2	3	4	5	6	7

What is the first day of the week?

_____

What day comes after Wednesday?

_____

What is the last day of the week?

_____

How many days are there in a week?

_____

Circle what day it is today.

Sunday Monday Tuesday Wednesday Thursday Friday Saturday

Days of the Week

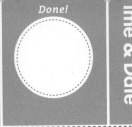

Done!

Put the days of the week in order by drawing a line from the day to its number.

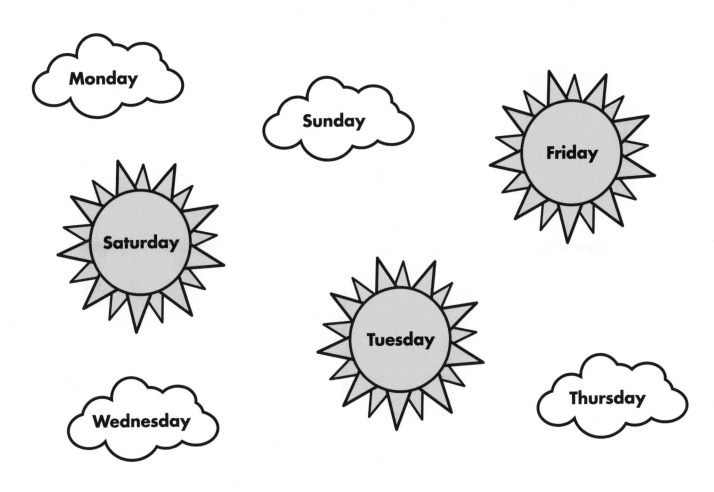

1	2	3	4	5	6	7

Circle what day it will be tomorrow.

Sunday Monday Tuesday Wednesday Thursday Friday Saturday

Done!

9, 10, 11, and 12

Practice writing numbers.

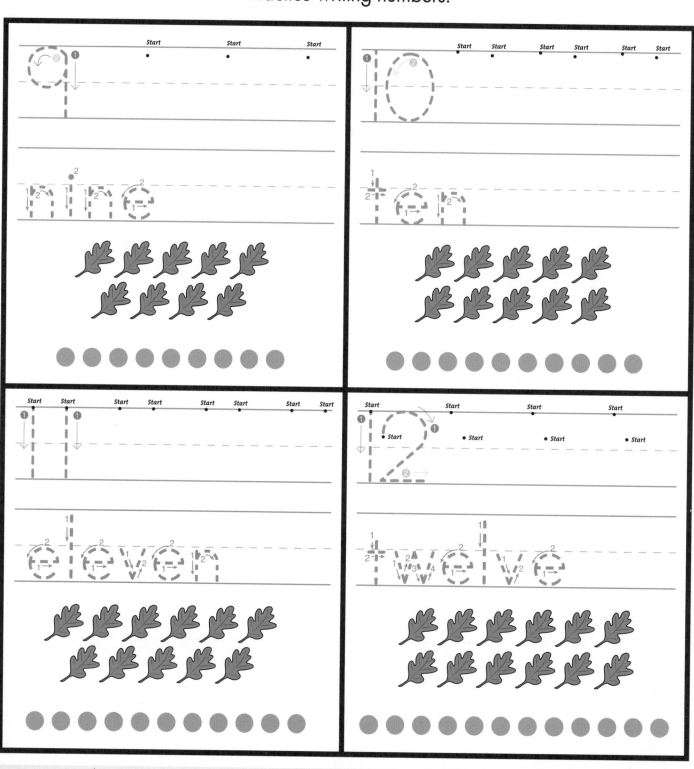

9, 10, 11, and 12

Tally marks are used to count or keep score. They are grouped in sets of five, which makes counting faster. Each **I** mark equals 1. After there are four **I** marks, a **/** mark crosses through them, which equals five.

1	 I	6	卌 I
2	II	7	卌 II
3	III	8	卌 III
4	IIII	9	卌 IIII
5	卌	10	卌 卌

Count the tally marks and circle the correct number.

卌 卌

9   10   11   12

卌 卌 II

9   10   11   12

Ordinal Numbers

Circle the 10th peanut. Draw a line under the 11th peanut.

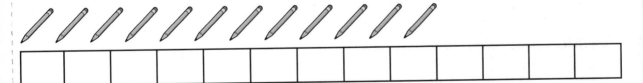

Count the pencils. Color a square for each pencil on the graph below.

SKIP COUNT BY
2's.

SAY THE NUMBERS OUT LOUD.

2
4
6
8
10
12

Months of the Year

There are 12 months in a year. Months are proper nouns and need to be **CAPITALIZED**.

January **1**	**F**ebruary **2**	**M**arch **3**	**A**pril **4**	**M**ay **5**	**J**une **6**
July **7**	**A**ugust **8**	**S**eptember **9**	**O**ctober **10**	**N**ovember **11**	**D**ecember **12**

What is the first month of the year? _____

In what month is your birthday? _____

What months are good to go to the pool? _____

What is the last month of the year? _____

What month comes after October? _____

Months of the Year

Done!

Look at the names of the months and write them in order.

Winter

December

January

February

Spring

March

April

May

Summer

June

July

August

Fall

September

October

November

Done!

13, 14, 15, and 16

Practice writing numbers.

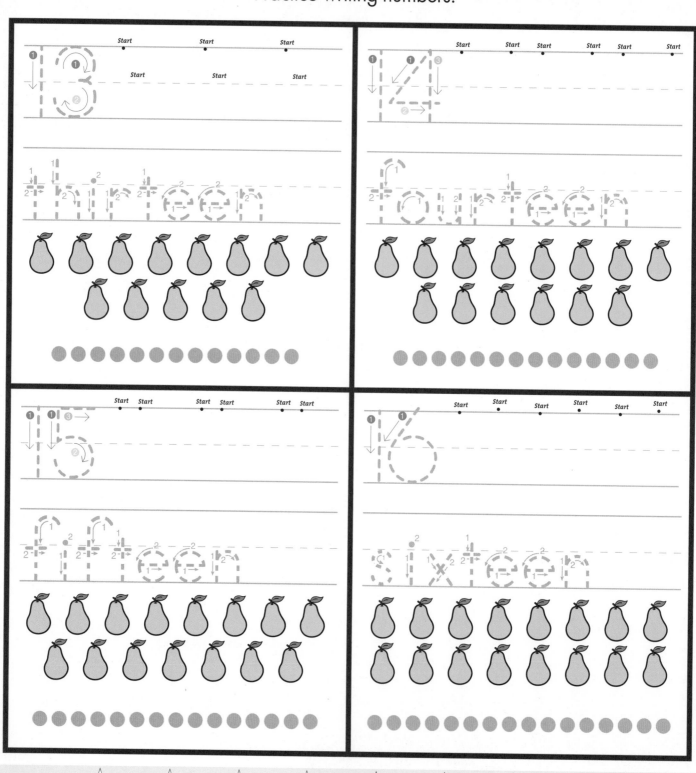

13, 14, 15, and 16

Tally marks are used to count or keep score. They are grouped in sets of five, which makes counting faster. Each **I** mark equals 1. After there are four **I** marks, a / mark crosses through them, which equals five.

1	 I	6	̷IIII I
2	II	7	̷IIII II
3	III	8	̷IIII III
4	IIII	9	̷IIII IIII
5	̷IIII	10	̷IIII ̷IIII

Count the tally marks and circle the correct number.

13   14   15   16   13   14   15   16

Ordinal Numbers

Circle the 14th whale. Draw a line under the 16th whale.

Color the robot with the smallest number.

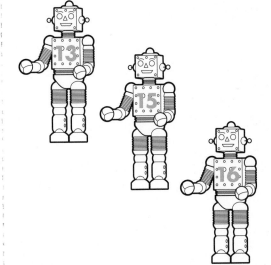

Write the smallest number.

_____

Write the largest number.

_____

SKIP COUNT BY.
2's.

SAY THE NUMBERS OUT LOUD.

2
4
6
8
10
12
14
16

10 11 12 13 14 15 16 17 18 19 20

★ 21 ★

Slow or Fast

A turtle is **slow**.

A turtle is **slower** than a rabbit.

A rabbit is **fast**.

A rabbit is **faster** than a turtle.

Circle the correct answer.

panther

cat

A panther is slower faster **than a cat.**

deer

cow

A deer is slower faster **than a cow.**

crab

shark

A crab is slower faster **than a shark.**

frog

worm

A frog is slower faster **than a worm.**

Left or Right

Trace the words **left** and **right** below. Now look at your hands and say which one is **left** and which one is **right**.

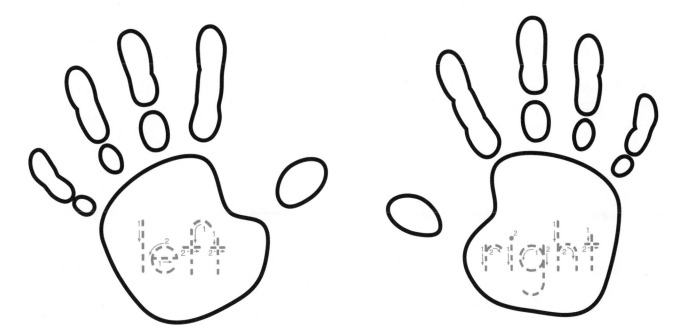

Color the apples on the **left** of the tree **green**.
Color the apples on the **right** of the tree **red**.

Fourth of July

The 4ᵗʰ of July is a day to celebrate America's birthday. It is the day we gained our independence from Britain.

Circle the symbol of America in each row that is different.

   (flags row with statue)

The Flag of the U.S.A.

The flag of the United States is a symbol of freedom.
Color in the letter **A red** and **B blue** the American flag below.

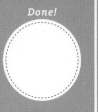
Learn the Pledge of Allegiance

Trace the missing words **the** in the Pledge below.

I pledge allegiance
to the flag of the
United States of America,
and to the republic
for which it stands,
one nation under God,
indivisible, with liberty
and justice for all.

Connect the dots from 1 to 10 in order. Then color the Liberty Bell.

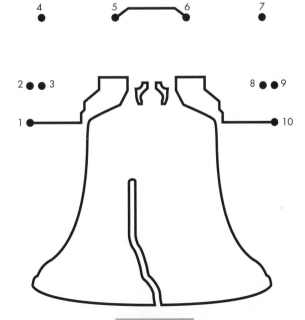

Practice writing numbers.

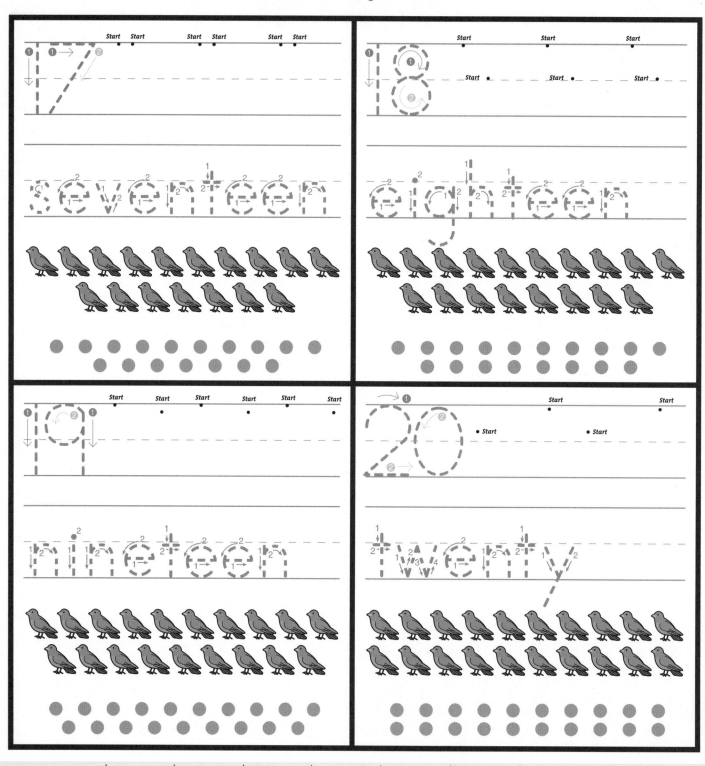

17, 18, 19, and 20

Tally marks are used to count or keep score. They are grouped in sets of five, which makes counting faster. Each **l** mark equals 1. After there are four **l** marks, a **/** mark crosses through them, which equals five.

1	 l	6	̶H̶H̶ l
2	ll	7	̶H̶H̶ ll
3	lll	8	̶H̶H̶ lll
4	llll	9	̶H̶H̶ llll
5	̶H̶H̶	10	̶H̶H̶ ̶H̶H̶

Count the tally marks and circle the correct number.

̶H̶H̶ ̶H̶H̶ ̶H̶H̶ ll   ̶H̶H̶ ̶H̶H̶ ̶H̶H̶ llll

17   18   19   20   **17   18   19   20**

Ordinal Numbers

Circle the 18th butterfly. Draw a line under the 20th butterfly.

Read the clues below. Draw a line from the clue to the correct answer.

17 **?** **This number is one greater than 18.** **?** **18**

? **?** **This number is one less than 19.** **?**

? **19** **This number is one greater than 16.** **20** **?**

What Time Is It?

Look at each of the clocks below. Write the correct time on the line provided. Remember, the short hand is the hour hand. The first has been done for you.

 **7** :00

 :00

 :00

 :00

 :00

 :00

 :00

 :00

 :00

School Time

Draw the hands on the clock to show what time school begins.

What Time Is It?

Look at each of the times below. Draw the hour hands on the clocks to show the correct time. The first has been done for you.

4:00

8:00

5:00

9:00

11:00

6:00

2:00

12:00

1:00

Sleep Time

Draw the hands on the clock to show your bedtime.

Count each item and add together. Write your answer on the line.

$1 + 3 =$ _____

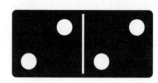

$2 + 2 =$ _____

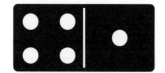

$4 + 1 =$ _____

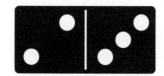

$2 + 3 =$ _____

Greater Than or Less Than

Alligators are hungry animals. They always want to eat the bigger number.
Think of the open end of the symbol **<** as the open mouth of an alligator
trying to eat the bigger number.

Now you try. Have the alligator eat the bigger number. Draw a **<** if the number
on the right is bigger or a **>** if the number on the left is bigger.

   1 ◯ 4   5 ◯ 2   3 ◯ 4

Count each group of shapes and add them together. Write your answer on the line.

2 + 3 = _____

4 + 1 = _____

1 + 3 = _____

2 + 2 = _____

Draw a line between each number and its name. Then draw a line between each number to the correct amount of objects.

three	3	
two	5	
four	1	
one	2	
five	4	

Done!

What Goes Together?

Look at the pictures in each row. Three of the items go together and one does not. Draw an **X** over the item that does not go with the rest.

What Goes Together?

Draw a line from the things on the left that go together with those on the right.

spider

 tractor

letters

 **fishbowl**

farmer

mailbox

fish

spiderweb

Draw something in the box below that goes with an umbrella.

Done!

Days of the Week

Find the names of the days of the week in the word search puzzle below.
The words go up, down and diagonal.

```
Y  L  M  O  N  D  A  Y  W  X
W  E  D  N  E  S  D  A  Y  V
N  P  M  A  X  M  Y  P  G  S
E  F  A  P  R  A  L  E  H  U
T  U  E  S  D  A  Y  K  C  N
B  U  C  I  F  I  V  M  E  D
E  T  R  A  G  W  E  N  M  A
J  F  S  A  T  U  R  D  A  Y
T  H  U  R  S  D  A  Y  E  E
```

Monday   Tuesday   Wednesday
Thursday   Friday   Saturday
Sunday

Circle what day it is today.

Sunday   Monday   Tuesday   Wednesday   Thursday   Friday   Saturday

Solve the riddle below by filling in the correct letter for each number.

1=A 2=B 3=C 4=D 5=E 6=F 7=G 8=H

9=I 10=J 11=K 12=L 13=M 14=N 15=O

16=P 17=Q 18=R 19=S 20=T 21=U

22=V 23=W 24=X 25=Y 26=Z

Can you name three days in a row without using the words Monday, Tuesday, Wednesday, Thursday, Friday, Saturday, or Sunday?

___ ___ ___ ___ ___ ___ ___ ___ ___,
25   5   19   20   5   18   4   1   25

___ ___ ___ ___ ___, and
20   15   4   1   25

___ ___ ___ ___ ___ ___ ___ ___!
20   15   13   15   18   18   15   23

Circle what day it was yesterday.

Sunday Monday Tuesday Wednesday Thursday Friday Saturday

Done!

6–10

Write these numbers in order from smallest to the largest.

6   10   2   4   □ □ □ □

1   8   5   4   □ □ □ □

7   3   9   1   □ □ □ □

Fill in the missing numbers in order.

1, ___, 3, 4

2, 3, ___, 5

7, 8, 9 ___

6, 7, ___, 9

4, ___, 6, 7

3, 4, 5, ___

Count the dots on each domino and add them together. Write your answers on the line.

_____ + _____ = _____

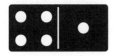   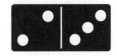

_____ + _____ = _____

_____ + _____ = _____

Greater Than or Less Than

Alligators are hungry animals. They always want to eat the bigger number.
Think of the open end of the symbol **<** as the open mouth of an alligator
trying to eat the bigger number.

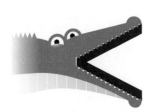 **3 < 6**    **4 > 2**

Now you try. Have the alligator eat the bigger number. Draw a **<** if the number
on the right is bigger or a **>** if the number on the left is bigger.

 **6 > 2**    **3 ◯ 8**   **10 ◯ 5**   **4 ◯ 9**

Done!

Find the Pattern

Look at the patterns below. Circle **yes** if the patterns are the same.
Circle **no** if the patterns are different.

1

Are these patterns the same?

Yes

No

2

Are these patterns the same?

Yes

No

3

Are these patterns the same?

Yes

No

Can You Find the Match?

All the snowmen are different except for two. Can you find the match?
Circle the two snowmen that are exactly the same.

Count the bugs below. Write the number of bugs in each row in the box.

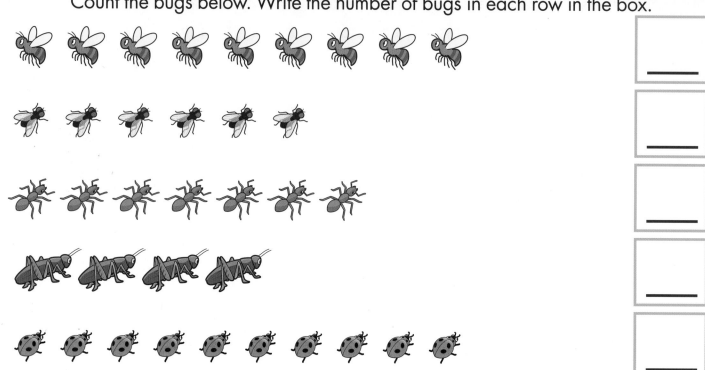

Are there more than in the row above? **Yes   No**

What bug is there the most of?

What bug is there the least of?

Skip-count by **5's**, **3's**, and **2's**. Fill in the missing numbers.

5
10
___

3
6
___
12

2
4
___

Draw a line between the matching numbers and the matching tally marks.

1

5

10

15

20

Fill in the missing numbers below.

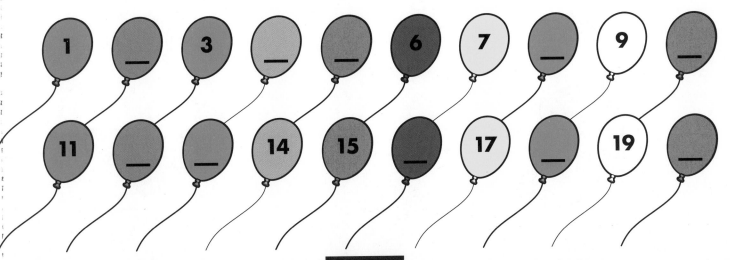

Match the Pictures That Rhyme

Draw a line from the picture on the left to the picture of the thing that rhymes with it on the right.

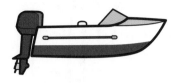

Words That Rhyme

Done!

Draw a line from each word on the left to the word that rhymes with it on the right.

 **corn**   **can**

 **school**   **wig**

 pig   **kite**

 **light**   **pool**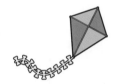

 **van**   **horn**

Happy Holidays

People celebrate many different holidays based on their beliefs.

What holiday do you celebrate in December?

Draw a picture of a decoration used during the holiday.

Draw a picture of a special food you eat during the holiday.

Make Your Own Snowflake

Cut out the snowflake below and decorate it any way you want.
Then hang it in your window!

Done!

1, 2, 3, and 4

Practice writing numbers.

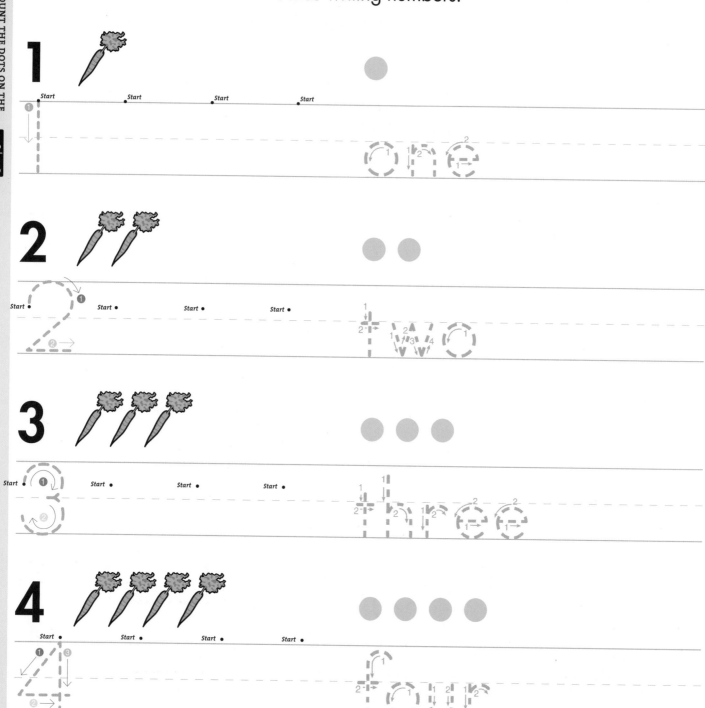

1, 2, 3, and 4

Done!

Ordinal Numbers

Color the 1st piece of chalk **red**. Color the 4th piece of chalk **yellow**.

Larger or Smaller

Color the fish with the larger number **orange**.

The **+** sign means you should add numbers together. Look at the groups below and count the number of animals in each one. Write the number on the lines provided and then add the two numbers together to get the sum or the total.

 _____ **+**  _____ **=** _____

 _____ **+** _____ **=** _____

 _____ **+**  _____ **=** _____

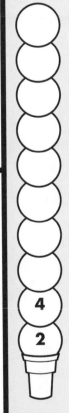

SKIP-COUNT BY

2's.

SAY THE NUMBERS OUT LOUD.

 10 11 12 13 14 15 16 17 18 19 20

Same Size

Circle the picture of the animal in each row that is the **same size** as the first picture.

Draw a circle in the box below the exact same size as the purple circle.

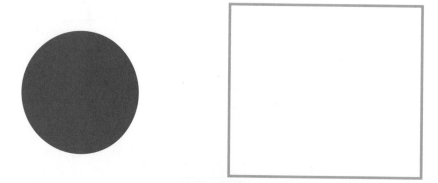

Different Size

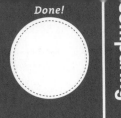

Circle the picture of the reptile in each row that is a **different size** than the first picture.

Done!

Telling Time

Look at the hands on each clock. Then draw a line to the box with its matching time. Remember, the small hand is the hour hand.

| 1:00 |
| 3:00 |
| 12:00 |

| 5:00 |
| 6:00 |
| 8:00 |

| 6:00 |
| 9:00 |
| 12:00 |

| 8:00 |
| 10:00 |
| 2:00 |

| 1:00 |
| 3:00 |
| 5:00 |

| 2:00 |
| 10:00 |
| 9:00 |

Telling Time

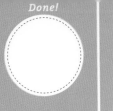

Look at the hands on each clock. Then draw a line to the clock with its matching time.

Done!

5, 6, 7, and 8

COUNT THE DOTS ON THE DOMINOES AND CIRCLE THE CORRECT NUMBER

5

6

7

8

Practice writing numbers.

5

Start • Start • Start •

6

Start • Start • Start •

7

Start • Start • Start •

8

Start • Start • Start •

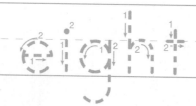

5, 6, 7, and 8

Ordinal Numbers

Color the 2ⁿᵈ and 6ᵗʰ car **red**. Color the 5ᵗʰ and 8ᵗʰ car **green**.

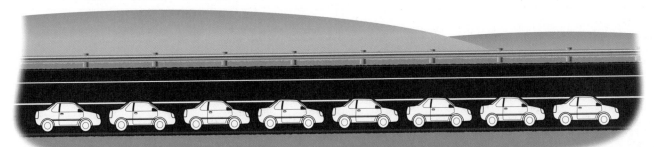

Larger or Smaller

Color the chick with the smaller number *yellow*.

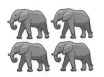 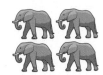

The **+** sign means you should add. Look at each of the groups below and count the number of animals. Write the correct amount on the lines provided and then add the two numbers together to get the sum or the total.

 _____ **+**  _____ **=** _____

 _____ **+** _____ **=** _____

_____ **+** _____ **=** _____

8
6
4
2

SKIP-COUNT BY

2's.

SAY THE NUMBER
OUT LOUD.

Days of the Week

Spell out the days of the week by filling in the missing letters.

> **Sunday Monday Tuesday Wednesday**
> **Thursday Friday Saturday**

Sun__a__

Mo__d____

T____sd__y

W__d__es____y

T__ur__d____

Fri____y

S__t__r__a__

Circle what day it is today.

Sunday Monday Tuesday Wednesday Thursday Friday Saturday

Days of the Week

Practice writing the days of the week.

Sunday	Monday	**Tuesday**	Wednesday
Thursday	Friday	**Saturday**	

Circle what day it will be tomorrow.

Sunday **Monday** Tuesday Wednesday **Thursday** **Friday** Saturday

Done!

9, 10, 11, and 12

Practice writing numbers.

9 Start Start Start

nine

10 Start Start Start Start Start Start

ten

11 Start Start Start Start Start Start Start Start

eleven

12 Start Start Start Start Start Start Start Start

twelve

9, 10, 11, and 12

Done!

Ordinal Numbers

Color in the 8th and 10th acorn **brown**. Color the 9th and 12th acorn orange.

Travis	Rob	Gray	Claire	Billy	Lila	Tim

Who is first?	Travis	Billy	Claire
Who is last?	Gray	Lila	Tim
Who is 6th?	Rob	Tim	Lila
Who is 5th?	Lila	Travis	Billy

3	10	9	6	7
5	12	11	9	12
12	10	8	10	12

How many 9's do you see? _____

How many 10's do you see? _____

How many 11's do you see? _____

How many 12's do you see? _____

12
10
8
6
4
2

SKIP-COUNT BY
2's.
SAY THE NUMBERS OUT LOUD.

| 10 | 11 | 12 | 13 | 14 | 15 | 16 | 17 | 18 | 19 | 20 |

Middle & Bottom

Top ······→

Middle ······→

Bottom ······→

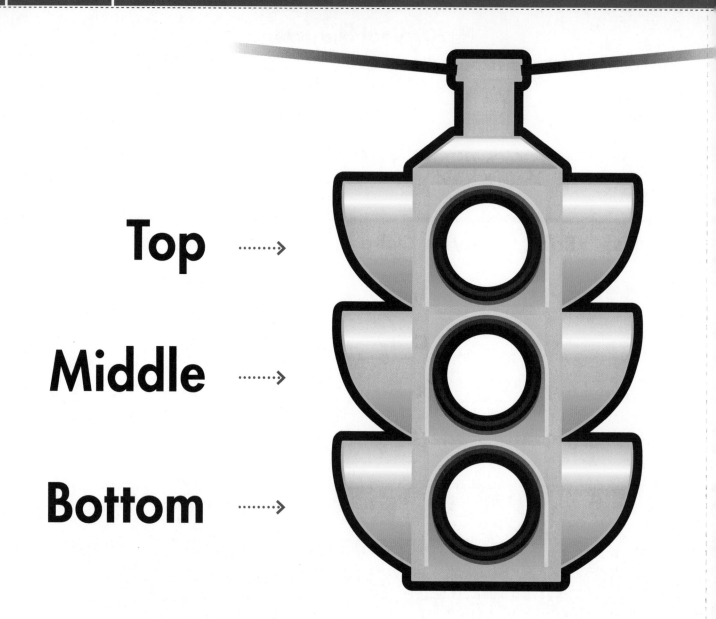

Color the top light **red**.

Color the middle light **yellow**.

Color the bottom light **green**.

Put an **X** under the shorter tree.

_____   _____

Color the **taller** animal.

Complete the sentence with either **short** or **tall**.

 **He is (short tall).**   **She is (short tall).**

Done!

13, 14, 15, and 16

13
14
15
16

Practice writing numbers.

13 Start Start Start

Start Start Start

thirteen

14 Start Start Start Start Start Start

fourteen

15 Start Start Start Start Start Start

fifteen

16 Start Start Start Start Start Start

sixteen

COLOR IN NUMBERS 13, 14, 15, AND 16.

1 2 3 4 5 6 7 8 9

13, 14, 15, and 16

Ordinal Numbers

Color the 13ᵗʰ and 15ᵗʰ apple **green**. Color the 14ᵗʰ and 16ᵗʰ apple **red**.

Larger or Smaller

Color the lily pad with the smaller number **green**.

Draw a line between each number and matching amount of bugs. Then draw a line between the bugs and the correct number of tally marks.

13

14

15

16

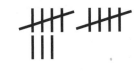

SKIP-COUNT BY
2's.
SAY THE NUMBERS
OUT LOUD.

10 11 12 13 14 15 16 17 18 19 20

In & Out

Trace the words **in** and **out**.

Write **in** or **out** in the following sentences.

The 🐦 is _____ the nest.

The 🕷 is _____ of the web.

The 🐿 is _____ the tree.

The 🦆 is _____ of the water.

The frog hops (**up**   **down**)

The frog sits (**up**   **down**)

The bear is (**up**   **down**) on the seesaw.

The fox is (**up**   **down**) on the seesaw.

Done!

Valentine's Day

Use the alphabet code to solve the secret message about Valentine's Day.

A=1　B=2　C=3　D=4　E=5　F=6　G=7　H=8

I=9　J=10　K=11　L=12　M=13　N=14　O=15

P=16　Q=17　R=18　S=19　T=20　U=21

V=22　W=23　X=24　Y=25　Z=26

___ ___ ___ ___　　___ ___ ___
23　9　12　12　　25　15　21

___ ___　　___ ___
2　5　　13　25

___ ___ ___ ___ ___ ___ ___ ___ ___
22　1　12　5　14　20　9　14　5

Make a Valentine

Make a Valentine for someone you love!
Cut out the heart below and then fill in the name of the person
you want to give it to. Don't forget to sign your own name!

To _____

I Love You!

From _____

Done!

17, 18, 19, and 20

COUNT THE DOTS ON THE DOMINOES AND CIRCLE THE CORRECT NUMBER

17
18
19
20

Practice writing numbers.

17   Start Start   Start Start   Start Start

seventeen

18   Start   Start   Start

Start   Start   Start

eighteen

19   Start   Start   Start   Start   Start   Start

nineteen

20   Start   Start

Start   Start

twenty

COLOR IN NUMBERS 17, 18, 19, AND 20.

1   2   3   4   5   6   7   8   9

Ordinal Numbers

Color in the 18th and 19th bone **brown**. Color in the 17th and 20th bone **black**.

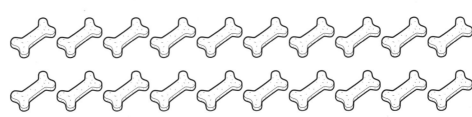

Larger or Smaller

Color the spider with the larger number **black**.

Fill in the missing numbers on the number lines below.

17 _____ **19** _____

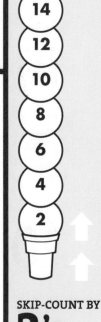

SKIP-COUNT BY
2's.

SAY THE NUMBERS
OUT LOUD.

Done!

Patterns

Look at the pictures below. There is a pattern in each row.
Once you have figured out the pattern, circle what comes next.

         or

         or

    **or**

        **or**

Patterns

Help the duck get to the pond by following the shape pattern ▲ ● ■ .

What Time Is It?

Look at each of the clocks below. Write the correct time on the line provided.
Remember, the small hand is the hour hand. The first one has been done for you.

8 :**00**

___ :**00**

___ :**00**

___ :**00**

___ :**00**

___ :**00**

___ :**00**

___ :**00**

___ :**00**

Lunchtime

Draw the hands on the clock to show what
time you eat lunch.

What Time Is It?

Look at each of the times below. Draw the hour hands on the clocks to show the correct time. The first one has been done for you.

5:00

7:00

3:00

10:00

12:00

6:00

1:00

11:00

4:00

Playtime

Draw the hands on the clock to show a time when you play.

Count the number of dots on each domino and then add together.
Write your answer on the line.

1 + 2 = _____

3 + 2 = _____

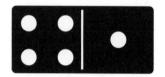

4 + 1 = _____

1 + 3 = _____

Greater Than or Less Than

Alligators are hungry animals. They always want to eat the bigger number.
Think of the open end of the symbol **<** as the open mouth of an alligator
trying to eat the bigger number.

1  3   4  2

Now you try. Have the alligator eat the bigger number. Draw a **<** if the number
on the right is bigger or a **>** if the number on the left is bigger.

4  1   2 ◯ 3   5 ◯ 4   2 ◯ 4

Draw the tally marks for each number.

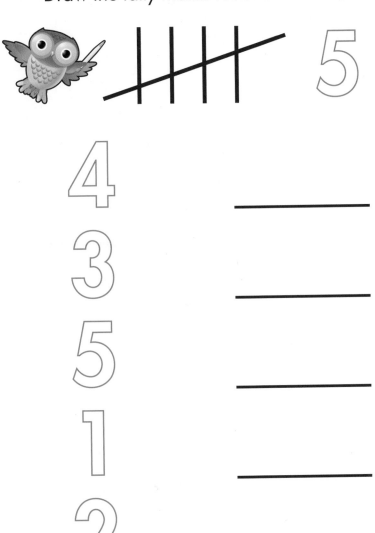

Ordinal Numbers

Circle the 2nd leaf. Draw a line under the 4th leaf.

Done!

Days of the Week

Draw a line from the day to its abbreviation.

Monday	Wed.
Tuesday	Fri.
Wednesday	Mon.
Thursday	Sat.
Friday	Tues.
Saturday	Sun.
Sunday	Thurs.

Circle what day it is today.

Sunday Monday Tuesday Wednesday Thursday Friday Saturday

Days of the Week

Spell out the days of the week by filling in the missing letters.

**Sunday Monday Tuesday Wednesday
Thursday Friday Saturday**

S__n__a__

M__nd____

__u__sday

__ed__es____y

T__ur__d____

__ri____y

S____ur__a__

Circle the last day in the week.

Sunday Monday Tuesday Wednesday Thursday Friday Saturday

Fill in the missing numbers from smallest to largest.

 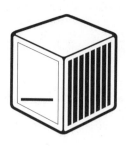  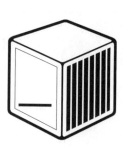 

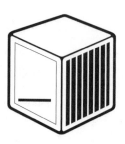  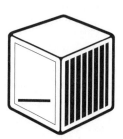  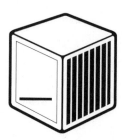

Write these numbers in order. Start with the smallest number.

5 9 3 4

2 10 6 7

8 2 9 1

1–10

Count the balls in each row. Write the number in the box.

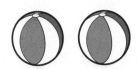

Are there more **than** **above?** **Yes** **No**

What ball is there the most of?

What ball is there the least of?

Done!

Find the Pattern

Look at the patterns in each column, running top to bottom.
Circle **yes** if the patterns are the same. Circle **no** if the patterns are different.

1

2

3

Are these patterns the same?

Yes   **No**

Are these patterns the same?

Yes   **No**

Are these patterns the same?

Yes   **No**

Can You Find the Match?

All of the socks below are different except for two. Can you find the match?
Circle the two socks that are exactly the same.

Done!

Months of the Year

Thirty Days Hath September (a poem)

Thirty days hath September,
April, June and November;
February has twenty eight alone,
All the rest have thirty-one.
Except in Leap Year, that's the time,
When February's days are twenty-nine.

January

S	M	T	W	T	F	S
1	2	3	4	5	6	7
8	9	10	11	12	13	14
15	16	17	18	19	20	21
22	23	24	25	26	27	28
29	30	31				

February

S	M	T	W	T	F	S
			1	2	3	4
5	6	7	8	9	10	11
12	13	14	15	16	17	18
19	20	21	22	23	24	25
26	27	28	29			

March

S	M	T	W	T	F	S
				1	2	3
4	5	6	7	8	9	10
11	12	13	14	15	16	17
18	19	20	21	22	23	24
25	26	27	28	29	30	31

April

S	M	T	W	T	F	S
1	2	3	4	5	6	7
8	9	10	11	12	13	14
15	16	17	18	19	20	21
22	23	24	25	26	27	28
29	30					

May

S	M	T	W	T	F	S
		1	2	3	4	5
6	7	8	9	10	11	12
13	14	15	16	17	18	19
20	21	22	23	24	25	26
27	28	29	30	31		

June

S	M	T	W	T	F	S
					1	2
3	4	5	6	7	8	9
10	11	12	13	14	15	16
17	18	19	20	21	22	23
24	25	26	27	28	29	30

July

S	M	T	W	T	F	S
1	2	3	4	5	6	7
8	9	10	11	12	13	14
15	16	17	18	19	20	21
22	23	24	25	26	27	28
29	30	31				

August

S	M	T	W	T	F	S
			1	2	3	4
5	6	7	8	9	10	11
12	13	14	15	16	17	18
19	20	21	22	23	24	25
26	27	28	29	30	31	

September

S	M	T	W	T	F	S
						1
2	3	4	5	6	7	8
9	10	11	12	13	14	15
16	17	18	19	20	21	22
23	24	25	26	27	28	29
30						

October

S	M	T	W	T	F	S
	1	2	3	4	5	6
7	8	9	10	11	12	13
14	15	16	17	18	19	20
21	22	23	24	25	26	27
28	29	30	31			

November

S	M	T	W	T	F	S
				1	2	3
4	5	6	7	8	9	10
11	12	13	14	15	16	17
18	19	20	21	22	23	24
25	26	27	28	29	30	

December

S	M	T	W	T	F	S
						1
2	3	4	5	6	7	8
9	10	11	12	13	14	15
16	17	18	19	20	21	22
23	24	25	26	27	28	29
30	31					

How many days are there in your birthday month?

What is the shortest month of the year?

How many days are in February during leap year?

Calendars

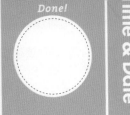

Calendars are a way to show the days of the week and the months of the year.
Calendars help us see all the days in a month or year at one time.
We use calendars to plan our time. Use the calendar below to answer the question.

February

M	T	W	T	F	S	S
				1	2	3
4	5	6	7	8	9	10
11	12	13	14	15	16	17
18	19	20	21	22	23	24
25	26	27	28			

Draw an **X** on February 10th.

What day is February 3rd?

Circle the last day of the month.

What is the date of the last Sunday of the month?

Read the clues below. Draw a line between the clue and the correct answer.

?

15

This number is one greater than 14.

?

20

This number is one greater than 19.

?

?

?

16 This number is one less than 17.

13

?

?

Skip-count by **2's**, **3's**, and **5's**.

2's 2 ___ 6 8 ___ 12 ___ ___ 18 ___

3's ___ 6 ___ 12 ___ 18

5's ___ 10 ___ 20

1–20

Done!

Fill in the missing numbers below.

1 __ 3 __ __ 6 __ 8 __ 10

11 __ 13 __ __ 16 __ 18 __ 20

Write these numbers in order, from smallest to largest.

6 10 2 12

16 18 5 14

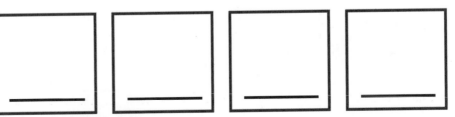

7 13 9 1

Match the Pictures That Rhyme

Draw a line from the picture on the left to the picture of the thing that rhymes with it on the right.

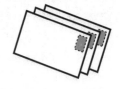

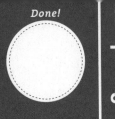

Draw a line from each word on the left to the word that rhymes with it on the right.

 **rug**

 **fruit**

 **sun**

 **fun**

 **dish**

  bug

ball

tall

 **suit**

fish

Thanksgiving

Cut along the dotted lines and then tape the sides of each pilgrim together to make two finger puppets!

Thanksgiving Day is a day for giving thanks. People give thanks with feasting and prayer for the blessings that they have received during the year.

What are **YOU** thankful for this year? Have your mom or dad help you write down what you are thankful for on the lines below.

Done!

1, 2, 3, and 4

Practice writing numbers.

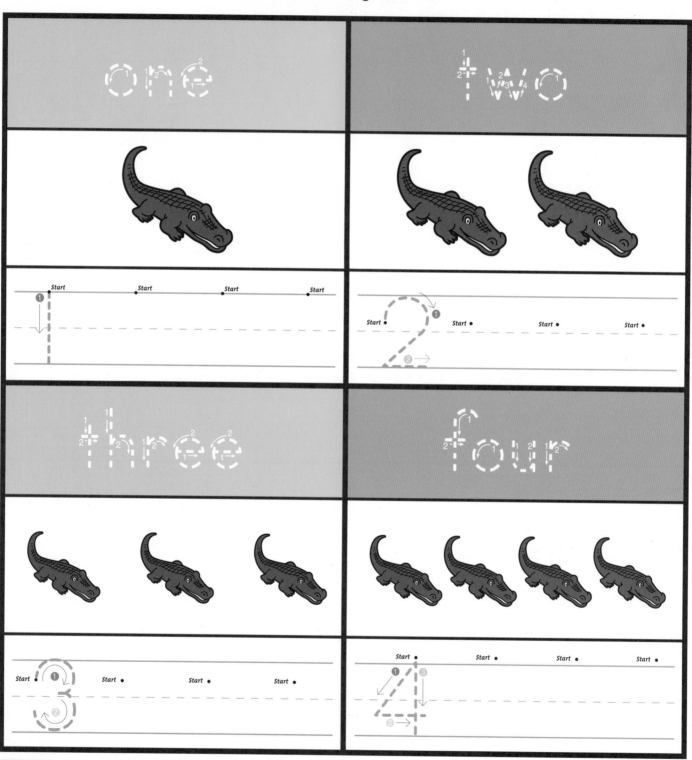

one

two

three

four

Start   Start   Start   Start

Start   Start   Start   Start

Start   Start   Start   Start

Start   Start   Start   Start

COLOR IN NUMBERS 1, 2, 3, AND 4.

| 1 | 2 | 3 | 4 | 5 | 6 | 7 | 8 | 9 | 10 |

1, 2, 3, and 4

By the Pond

How many are there? Count the objects and circle the correct number.

ducks		1	3	4
kites		1	2	3
lilly pads		2	3	4
butterflies		1	2	4

Fill in the graph by coloring the spaces to show how many objects you counted.

	1	2	3	4

Which one was there most of?

11 12 13 14 15 16 17 18 19 20

SKIP-COUNT BY
2's.
SAY THE NUMBERS OUT LOUD.

Same Size

Look at the picture of the socks in each row. Circle the picture of the sock in each row that is the **same size** as the first picture.

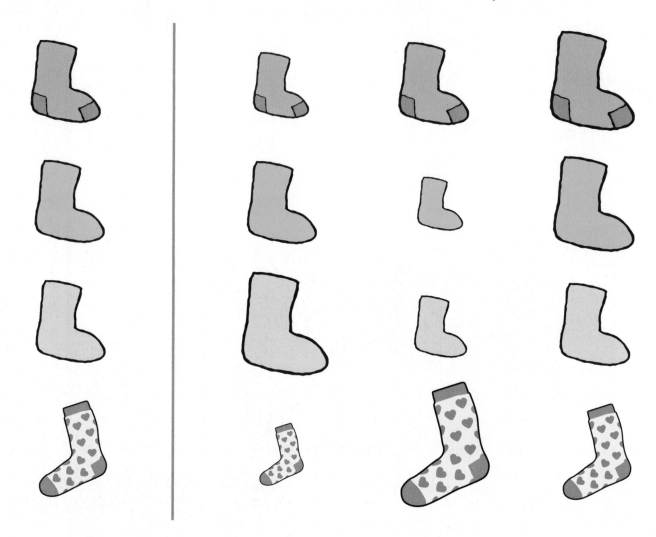

Draw a square in the box the exact same size as the purple square.

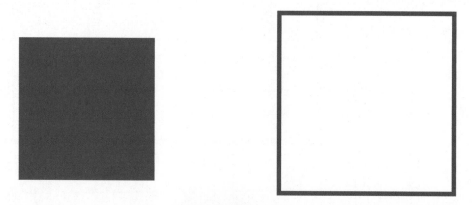

Different Size

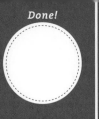

Done!

Look at the picture of the bugs in each row. Circle the picture of the one bug in each row that is a **different size** than the first picture.

 |

 |

 |

 |

Done!

5, 6, 7, and 8

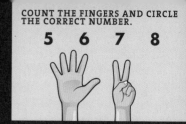

Practice writing numbers.

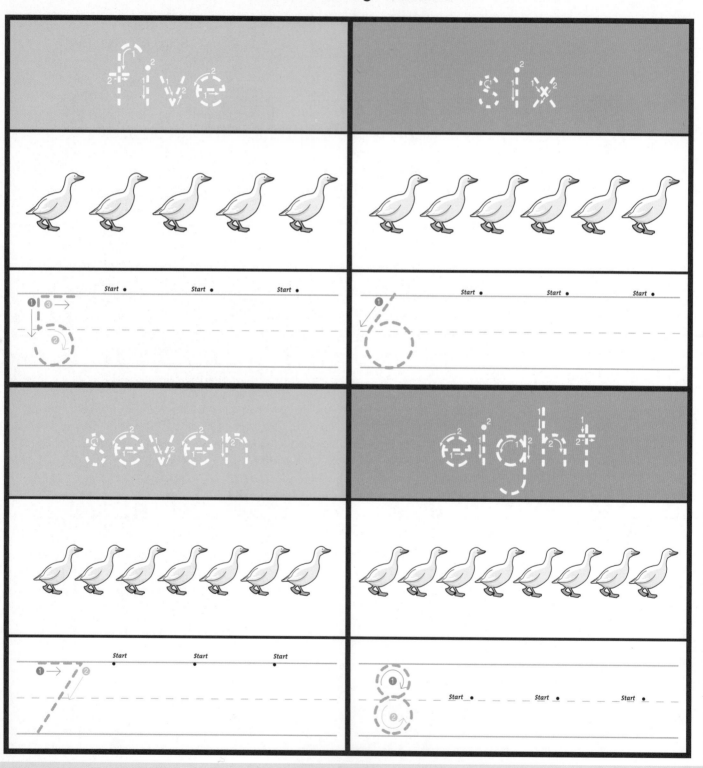

five

six

seven

eight

Start • Start • Start •

Start • Start • Start •

Start • Start • Start

Start • Start • Start •

COLOR IN NUMBERS 5, 6, 7, AND 8.

 1   **2**   **3**   **4**   **5**   **6**   **7**   **8**   **9**   **10**

The **+** sign means you should add. Look at each of the groups below and count the number of animals in each one. Write the correct number on the lines provided and then add the two numbers together to get the sum or the total.

 _____ **+**  _____ **=** _____

 _____ **+**  _____ **=** _____

 _____ **+**  _____ **=** _____

Draw a line from the number to its matching number of bugs. Then draw a line from the group of bugs to that number's tally mark.

5   🕷🕷🕷🕷🕷🕷🕷   ⅢⅡ I

6   🪰🪰🪰🪰🪰   ⅢⅡ III

7   🐝🐝🐝🐝🐝🐝   ⅢⅡ

8   🐜🐜🐜🐜🐜🐜🐜🐜   ⅢⅡ II

11 **12** **13** **14** **15** **16** **17** **18** **19** **20**

Done!

Bigger and Smaller

Look at the objects in each box and color in the one that is **bigger**.

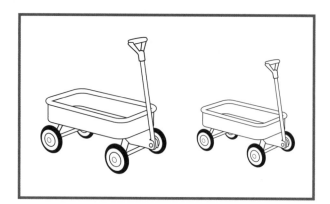

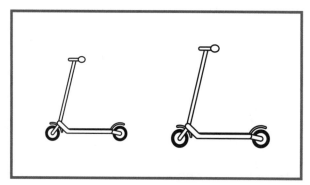

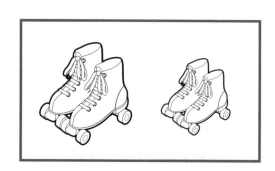

Look at the objects in each box and color in the one that is **smaller**.

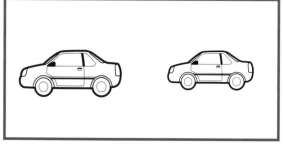

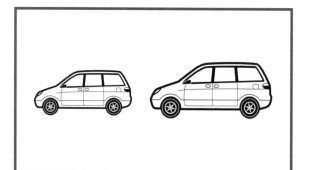

Draw an **X** through the **biggest** animal and **circle** the **smallest** animal in each row.

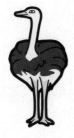  

9, 10, 11, and 12

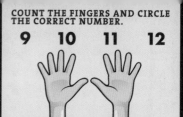

Practice writing numbers.

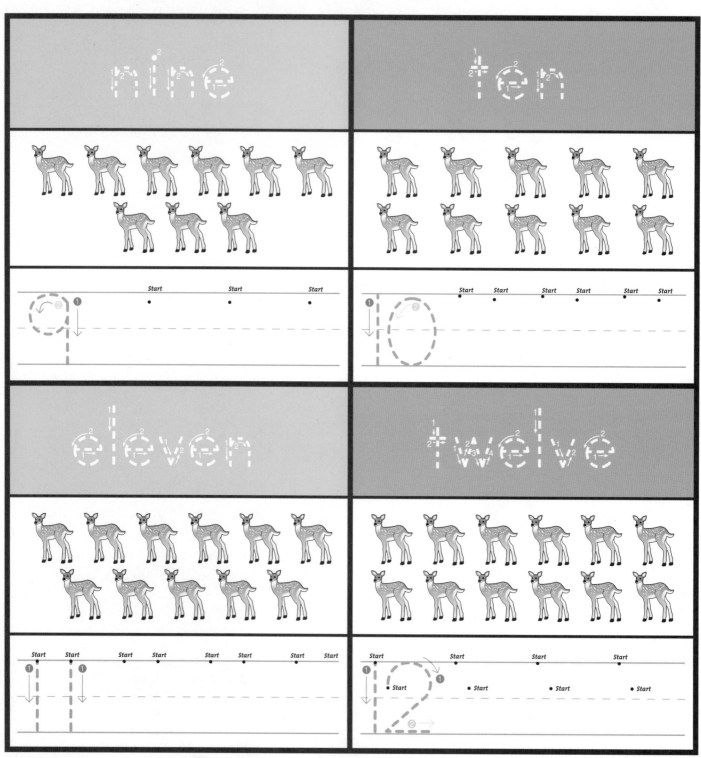

nine

ten

eleven

twelve

Start   Start   Start

Start   Start   Start   Start   Start   Start

Start   Start   Start   Start   Start   Start   Start   Start

Start   Start   Start   Start

Start   Start   Start   Start

COLOR IN
NUMBERS
9, 10, 11, AND 12.

1   2   3   4   5   6   7   8   9   10

Fill in the missing numbers on the number lines below.

9   _____   **11**   _____

SKIP-COUNT BY

2's.

SAY THE NUMBERS OUT LOUD.

 2

 4

 6

 8

 10

 12

Count the shells on the beach. Fill in the boxes of the graph to show the amount of shells.

Circle which shell has more:

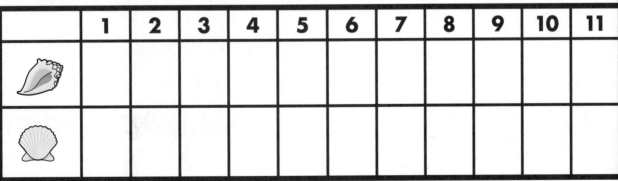

	1	2	3	4	5	6	7	8	9	10	11

(11) (12) (13) (14) (15) (16) (17) (18) (19) (20)

Done!

Wet or Dry

Look at the picture and then circle whether the animal that lives in a **wet** or **dry** environment.

wet **dry**

wet **dry**

wet **dry**

wet **dry**

wet **dry**

wet **dry**

Hot or Cold

Draw a line from each picture to the thermometer that is either **hot** or **cold**.

COLD

HOT

Done!

Months of the Year

Find and circle the months of the year in the word search below
by looking up, down or diagonally.

```
J A N U A R Y H W X
U F E B R U A R Y V
N O V E M B E R D E
E F A P R I L E E O
M A R C H N B K C C
B U C M F I V M E T
E T H A G W E N M O
J U L Y H A I T B B
F K O I G H Z J E E
S E P T E M B E R R
F A U G U S T Y C B
```

January **February** **March**
April **May** **June** **July** **August**
September **October**
November **December**

Months of the Year

The four seasons are: **Winter** Spring Summer **Fall**

January	**F**ebruary	**M**arch	**A**pril	**M**ay	**J**une
July	**A**ugust	**S**eptember	**O**ctober	**N**ovember	**D**ecember

Winter

J_ _ _ _ _ _ _

_ eb _ _ _ _ _ _

M _ _ _ _ _

Spring

A _ _ _ _ _ _

_ ay

J _ _ _ e

Summer

_ ul _

A _ _ _ _ _ _ t

S _ pt _ _ _ _ _

Fall

O _ t _ _ _ _ _

_ _ vem _ _ _ _

D _ _ em _ _ _

Done!

13, 14, 15, and 16

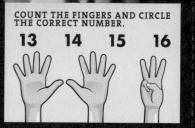

Practice writing numbers.

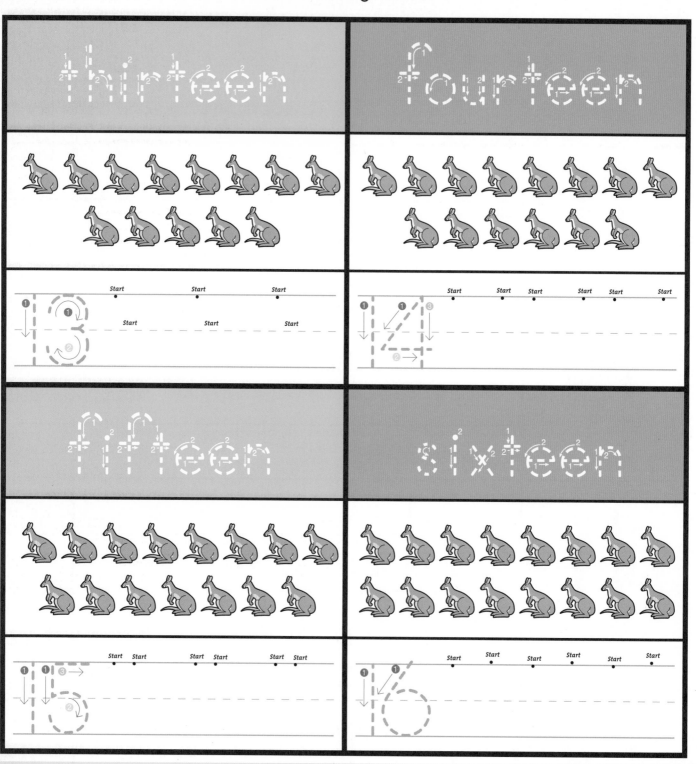

thirteen

fourteen

Start   Start   Start

Start   Start   Start

fifteen

sixteen

Start   Start   Start   Start   Start   Start

Start   Start   Start   Start   Start   Start

| 1 | 2 | 3 | 4 | 5 | 6 | 7 | 8 | 9 | 10 |

13, 14, 15, and 16

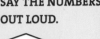

16	13	15	6	7
5	16	14	9	15
15	13	8	13	15

How many 13's do you see? _____

How many 14's do you see? _____

How many 15's do you see? _____

How many 16's do you see? _____

SKIP-COUNT BY **2's.**

SAY THE NUMBERS OUT LOUD.

 2

 4

 6

 8

 10

 12

 14

 16

Color the snowman with the smallest number.

Write the smallest number.

_____

Write the largest number.

_____

Read the clues below. Draw a line from the clue to the correct answer.

13   **The number is one greater than 13.**   **15**

?   **?**   **The number is one less than 16.**   **?**   **?**

14   **The number is one less than 14.**   **16**

(11) (12) (13) (14) (15) (16) (17) (18) (19) (20)

Over & Under

Trace the words **over** and **under**.

The bee is **over** the flower.

The worm is **under** the flower.

Color the spider **over** the web **black**. Color the spider **under** the web **brown**.

Full & Empty

Look at each picture. Draw a line from the **full** box to each of the items that are **full**. Then draw a line from the **empty** box to each of the items that are **empty**.

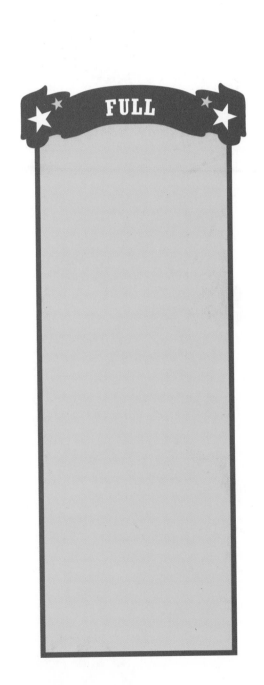

FULL

EMPTY

Done!

Halloween

Make your own jack-o-lantern! Cut along the dotted lines and then color it in.

Halloween

Use the alphabet code to solve the secret riddle.

A=1 B=2 C=3 D=4 E=5 F=6 G=7 H=8

I=9 J=10 K=11 L=12 M=13 N=14 O=15

P=16 Q=17 R=18 S=19 T=20 U=21

V=22 W=23 X=24 Y=25 Z=26

What was the favorite game at the ghosts' birthday party?

___ ___ ___ ___
8   9   4   5

___ ___ ___
1 14 4

___ ___ ___ ___ ___ ___
19 8 18 9 5 11

Done!

17, 18, 19, and 20

Practice writing numbers.

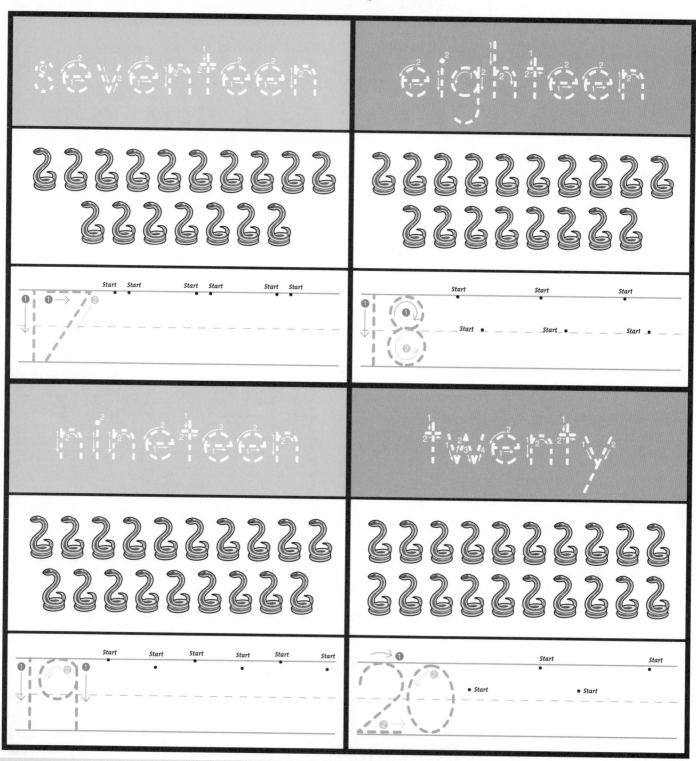

Larger or Smaller

Color the birthday cake with the smaller number **pink**.
Color the birthday cake with the larger number **yellow**.

Ordinal Numbers

Color in the 17th and 18th sun **yellow**.
Color in the 19th and 20th sun **orange**.

1 2 3 4 5 6 7 8 9 10

11 12 13 14 15 16 17 18 19 20

Draw a line from the number to the matching spelled out numbers and then to its tally mark.

17   **twenty** ||||| ||||| ||||| ||||

18   **nineteen** ||||| ||||| ||||| |||||

19   **seventeen** ||||| ||||| ||||| |||

20   **eighteen** ||||| ||||| ||||| ||

11 12 13 14 15 16 17 18 19 20

SKIP-COUNT BY
2's.
SAY THE NUMBERS OUT LOUD.

2

4

6

8

10

12

14

16

18

20

Patterns

Look at the pictures below. There is a pattern in each row.
Once you have figured out the pattern, circle what comes next.

 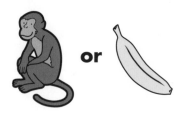

 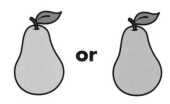

 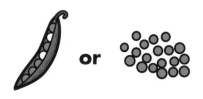

Shape Patterns

Help the frog get to the lily pad by following this shape pattern ● ■ ♥.

Done!

1–5

Count the tools and write the number in the box.

Which tool do you have the most of?

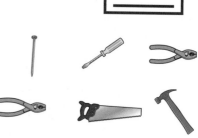

Which tool do you have the least of?

Count the dots on each domino and add them together. Write your answer on the line.

3 + 2 = _____

1 + 1 = _____

2 + 1 = _____

2 + 2 = _____

Look at the numbers in each row below and finish the pattern

1   2   3   1   2   _____

3   4   3   4   3   _____

1   2   1   2   1   _____

Find the numbers in the word search below.

Z E L T H R E E K X
F O U R O T L I M V
J K T A X M L H N E
E O O N I N P J T R
N P N D O N B P W T
B F E A F I V E O Y

ONE   TWO   THREE   FOUR   FIVE

Done!

Things That Go Together

Look at the pictures in each row. Three of the items go together and one does not. Draw an **X** over the item that does not go with the rest.

Draw a line from the object in the left column to the object in the right column it goes with.

cake

 **knife**

brush

 shirt

pants

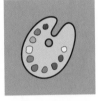 paint

fork

 candle

Draw something in the box that goes with a scarf.

Mother's Day

Mother's Day is to celebrate what a fantastic **mother** you have and to thank her for all the nice things that she does for you.

Draw a picture of you and your mom in the frame below.
Then cut it out along the dotted line and give it to her as a gift!

Father's Day

Done!

Father's Day is to celebrate what a great dad you have and how special he is to you.

Cut out and decorate the hand below. Then give it to your dad to show him how much you care. Don't forget to sign it!

#1 DAD

Love,

1–10

Greater Than or Less Than

Alligators are hungry animals. They always want to eat the bigger number. Think of the open end of the symbol **<** as the open mouth of an alligator trying to eat the bigger number.

 **1**  **< 3**   **4 >** **2**

Now you try. Have the alligator eat the bigger number. Draw a **<** if the number on the right is bigger or a **>** if the number on the left is bigger.

4 (>) 2   6 ( ) 10   8 ( ) 4   3 ( ) 9

6 ( ) 1   8 ( ) 10   9 ( ) 7   6 ( ) 7

Write these numbers in order from smallest to largest.

3   6   4   9

9   2   5   1

8   7   10   2

Circle the correct number of vehicles in each row.

4   **6**   **8**   **10**

1   **3**   **6**   **9**

1   **4**   **6**   **8**

2   **4**   **8**   **10**

3   **5**   **8**   **10**

Read the clues below. Draw a line from the clue to the correct answer.

?

3

5   **?**

The number is one greater than 2.

The number is one less than 9.

7   **?**   The number is one less than 6   **8**   **?**

?

Find the Patterns

Look at the patterns in each column below. Circle **yes** if the two patterns in each column are the same. Circle **no** if the two patterns in each column are different.

1

Are these patterns the same?

Yes   **No**

2

Are these patterns the same?

Yes   **No**

3

Are these patterns the same?

Yes   **No**

Can You Find the Match?

All of the spinning tops are different except for two. Can you find the match?
Circle the two spinning tops that are exactly the same.

Done!

Months of the Year

Draw a line from the months to their abbreviations.

 January

Oct.

 February

Nov.

 March

Sept.

 April

Jul.

 May

Aug.

 June

May

 July

Feb.

 August

Dec.

 September

Jan.

 October

Mar.

 November

Apr.

 December

Jun.

What Month Is It?'

Done!

Draw a line from each month to its holiday.

Independence Day

Valentine's Day

Thanksgiving

Christmas

New Year's Day

Halloween

January
M	T	W	T	F	S	S
	1	2	3	4	5	6
7	8	9	10	11	12	13
14	15	16	17	18	19	20
21	22	23	24	25	26	27
28	29	30	31			

October
M	T	W	T	F	S	S
	1	2	3	4	5	6
7	8	9	10	11	12	13
14	15	16	17	18	19	20
21	22	23	24	25	26	27
28	29	30	31			

February
M	T	W	T	F	S	S
				1	2	3
4	5	6	7	8	9	10
11	12	13	14	15	16	17
18	19	20	21	22	23	24
25	26	27	28			

November
M	T	W	T	F	S	S
				1	2	3
4	5	6	7	8	9	10
11	12	13	14	15	16	17
18	19	20	21	22	23	24
25	26	27	28	29	30	

July
M	T	W	T	F	S	S
1	2	3	4	5	6	7
8	9	10	11	12	13	14
15	16	17	18	19	20	21
22	23	24	25	26	27	28
29	30	31				

December
M	T	W	T	F	S	S
						1
2	3	4	5	6	7	8
9	10	11	12	13	14	15
16	17	18	19	20	21	22
23	24	25	26	27	28	29

1–20

Fill in the missing numbers.

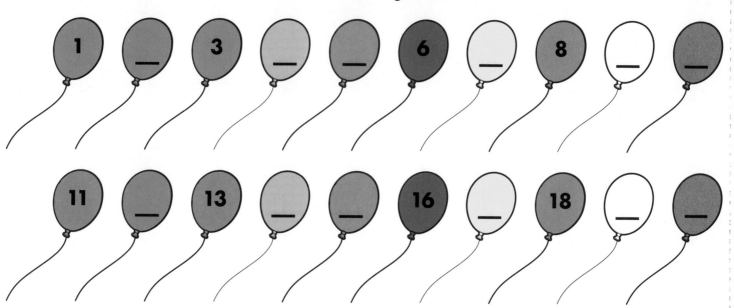

1 __ 3 __ __ 6 __ 8 __ __

11 __ 13 __ __ 16 __ 18 __ __

Help the bird get to her egg by following the numbers **1** to **20** in order.

		1	2	3	4	5	20	4
		11	5	6	2	6	4	18
3	7	3	8	19	10	7	17	2
4	4	12	11	10	9	8	3	1
18	9	13	9	13	6	3	15	11
5	2	14	12	20	2	16		
2	13	15	5	8	1	2		
9	7	16	17	18	19	20		
1	5	19	3	11	14	4		

Skip-count by **2's**, **3's**, and **5's**.

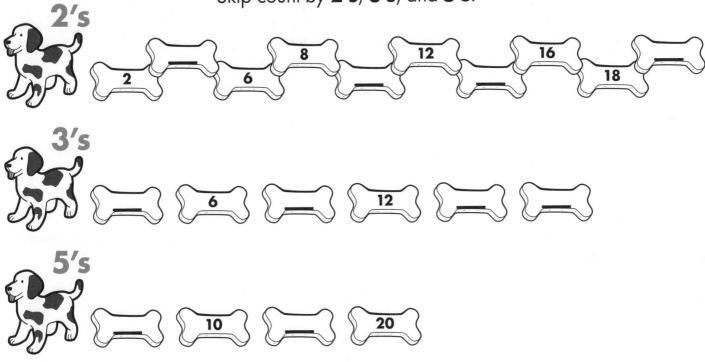

2's

2 ___ 6 8 ___ 12 ___ 16 18 ___

3's

___ 6 ___ 12 ___ ___

5's

___ 10 ___ 20

Count the number of sea creatures then color the correct number below.

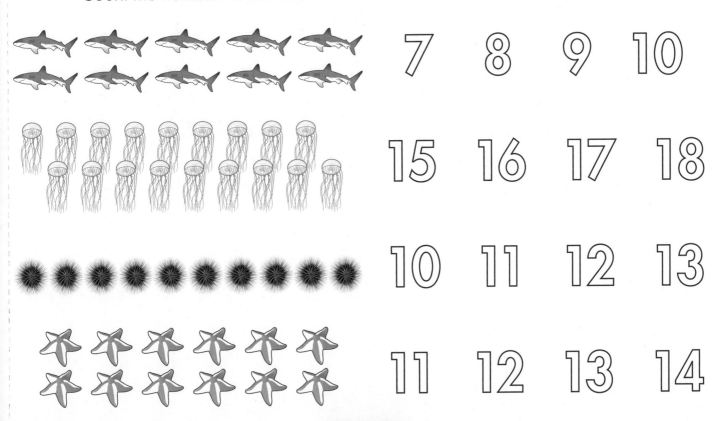

7　8　9　10

15　16　17　18

10　11　12　13

11　12　13　14

Page 5

Page 12

Page 21

Page 29
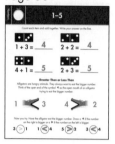

Page 35

Page 6

Page 13

Page 22

Page 30

Page 36
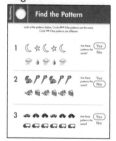

Page 7

Page 14

Page 24

Page 31
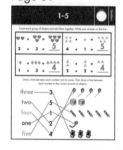

Page 37

Page 8

Page 15

Page 25

Page 32

Page 38

Page 9

Page 17

Page 27

Page 33
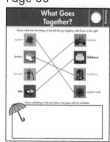

Page 39

Page 11

Page 18

Page 28

Page 34

Page 40

126 **ANSWERS** ★

Page 41
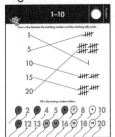
1–10

Page 50
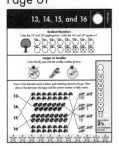
Telling Time

Page 61
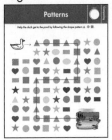
13, 14, 15, and 16

Page 69

Patterns

Page 75

Days of the Week

Page 42

Match the Pictures That Rhyme

Page 51
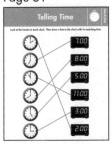
Telling Time

Page 62
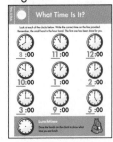
In & Out

Page 70

What Time Is It?

Page 76
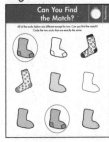
1–10

Page 43
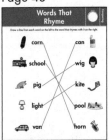
Words That Rhyme

Page 53

5, 6, 7, and 8

Page 63

Up & Down

Page 71

What Time Is It?

Page 77
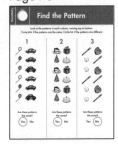
1–10

Page 47

1, 2, 3, and 4

Page 54

Days of the Week

Page 64

Valentine's Day

Page 72
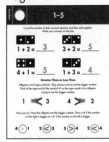
1–5

Page 78

Find the Pattern

Page 48

Same Size

Page 57

9, 10, 11, and 12

Page 67
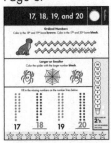
17, 18, 19, and 20

Page 73
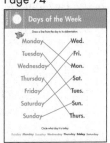
1–5

Page 79
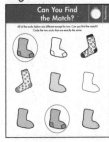
Can You Find the Match?

Page 49

Different Size

Page 59

Short & Tall

Page 68
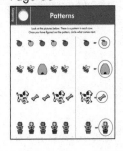
Patterns

Page 74
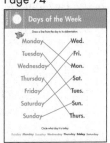
Days of the Week

Page 80

Months of the Year

Page 81

Calendars

February

What day is February 3rd?
Sunday

Circle the last day of the month.

What is the date of the last Sunday of the month?
24

Page 90

Same Size

Page 98

Wet or Dry

wet (dry) wet (dry)

wet (dry) (wet) dry

wet (dry) wet (dry)

Page 107

Halloween

A=1 B=2 C=3 D=4 E=5 F=6 G=7 H=8
I=9 J=10 K=11 L=12 M=13 N=14 O=15
P=16 Q=17 R=18 S=19 T=20 U=21
V=22 W=23 X=24 Y=25 Z=26

H I D E
8 9 4 5

A N D
1 14 4

S H R I E K
19 8 18 9 5 11

Page 114

Things That Go Together

Page 122
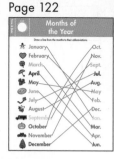

Months of the Year

January — Oct.
February — Nov.
March — Sept.
April — Jul.
May — Aug.
June — May
July — Feb.
August — Dec.
September — Jan.
October — Mar.
November — Apr.
December — Jun.

Page 82

1–20

15 — this number is one greater than 14.
? — this number is one greater than 19. — **20**
16 — this number is one less than 12. — **13**

Page 91

Different Size

Page 99
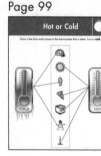

Hot or Cold

COLD   HOT

Page 109

17, 18, 19, and 20

Larger or Smaller

Ordinal Numbers

twenty
nineteen
seventeen
eighteen

11 12 13 14 15 16 17 18 19 20

Page 115

Things That Go Together

comb — knife
brush — shirt
pencil — paint
fork — candle

Page 123

What Month Is It?'

Independence Day
Valentine's Day
Thanksgiving
Christmas
New Year's Day
Halloween

Page 83

1–20

Fill in the missing numbers below.
12 13 14 15 16

Write these numbers in order, from smallest to largest.
6 10 2 12 → 2 6 10 12
16 18 5 14 → 5 14 16 18
7 13 9 1 → 1 7 9 13

Page 93

5, 6, 7, and 8

4 + 2 = 6
3 + 4 = 7
6 + 2 = 8

Page 100

Months of the Year

J A N U A R Y H W X
U E B R U A R Y O V
N O V E M B E R D C
E F A P R I L E K T
M A R C H E B E M O
B U C M H J A V E B
E T H A G V E N R E
J U L Y H A I T P R
N F O O J D H C J E
S E P T E M B E R Z
F A U G U S T G O Y

January February March
April May June July August
September **October**
November **December**

Page 110

Patterns

Page 118

1–10

Greater Than or Less Than

4 < 6 7 > 2

3 6 4 9 → 3 4 6 9
9 2 5 1 → 1 2 5 9
8 7 10 2 → 2 7 8 10

Page 124

1–20

Fill in the missing numbers.
2 4 5 7 9 10
12 14 15 17 19 20

1 2 3 4 5
11 12 13 14 15
1 2 3 4 5
11 12 13 14 15

Page 84

Match the Pictures That Rhyme

Page 94

Bigger and Smaller

Page 101

Months of the Year

January
February
March
April
May
June
July
August
September
October
November
December

Page 111

Shape Patterns

Page 119

1–10

4 (6) 8 10
1 (3) 6 9
1 4 6 (8)
(2) 4 8 10
3 5 8 (10)

Page 125

1–20

7 8 9 (10)
15 16 17 (18)
(10) 11 12 13
11 (12) 13 14

Page 85

Words That Rhyme

rug — fruit
sun — fun
dish — bug
ball — tall
suit — fish

Page 95

Bigger and Smaller

Page 103

13, 14, 15, and 16

How many 13's do you see? **3**
How many 14's do you see? **4**
How many 15's do you see? **?**
How many 16's do you see? **2**

Write the smallest number. **13**
Write the largest number. **16**

11 12 13 14 15 16 17 18 19 20

Page 112

1–5

3 + 2 = 5
1 + 1 = 2
2 + 2 = 4

Page 120

Find the Patterns

Yes No Yes

Page 89

1, 2, 3, and 4

Page 97

9, 10, 11, and 12

9 10 11 12

Page 105

Full & Empty

FULL   EMPTY

Page 113

1–5

2 3 3
3 4 4
1 1 2

Z E L T H R E E K X
F O U R O T L I M V
J K T A X M L H N E
E O O N I N P J T R
N P N D O N B P W T
B E F I V E O Y

ONE TWO THREE **FOUR** FIVE

Page 121

Can You Find the Match?

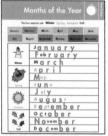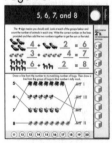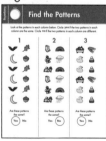

128 ANSWERS ★

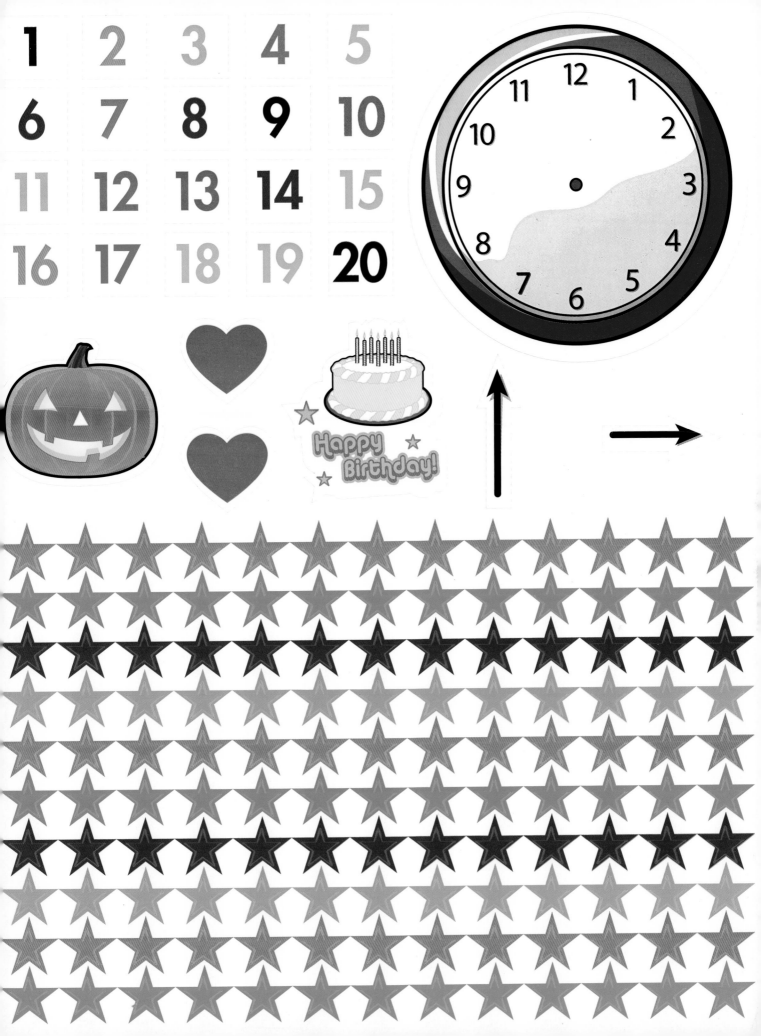